W9-BZX-301

RAMSES II

EGYPTIAN PHARAOH, WARRIOR, AND BUILDER

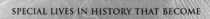

SPECIAL LIVES IN HISTORY THAT BECOME

Signature LIVES

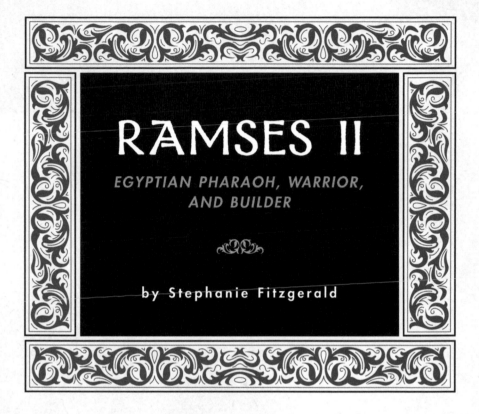

RAMSES II

EGYPTIAN PHARAOH, WARRIOR, AND BUILDER

by Stephanie Fitzgerald

Content Adviser: Jennifer Houser Wegner, Ph.D.,
Egyptian Section,
University of Pennsylvania Museum

Reading Adviser: Rosemary G. Palmer, Ph.D.,
Department of Literacy, College of Education,
Boise State University

Compass Point Books ✦ Minneapolis, Minnesota

Compass Point Books
151 Good Counsel Drive
P.O. Box 669
Mankato, MN 56002-0669

Copyright © 2009 by Compass Point Books
All rights reserved. No part of this book may be reproduced without written permission
from the publisher. The publisher takes no responsibility for the use of any of the
materials or methods described in this book, nor for the products thereof.
Printed in the United States of America.

This book was manufactured with paper containing at least
10 percent post-consumer waste.

Editor: Anthony Wacholtz
Page Production: Ashlee Suker
Photo Researcher: Svetlana Zhurkin
Cartographer: XNR Productions, Inc.
Library Consultant: Kathleen Baxter

Art Director: LuAnn Ascheman-Adams
Creative Director: Keith Griffin
Editorial Director: Nick Healy
Managing Editor: Catherine Neitge

Library of Congress Cataloging-in-Publication Data
Fitzgerald, Stephanie.
  Ramses II : Egyptian pharaoh, warrior, and builder / by Stephanie
Fitzgerald.
      p. cm—(Signature lives)
  Includes bibliographical references and index.
  ISBN 978-0-7565-3836-1 (library binding)
1. Ramses II, King of Egypt—Juvenile literature. 2. Egypt—History—
Nineteenth dynasty, ca. 1320–1200 B.C.—Juvenile literature.
3. Pharaohs—Biography—Juvenile literature. I. Title. II. Series.
  DT88.F585 2008
  932'.014092—dc22   2008005726

Visit Compass Point Books on the Internet at *www.compasspointbooks.com*
or e-mail your request to *custserv@compasspointbooks.com*

Signature Lives

ANCIENT WORLD

Societies of long ago were peopled with unique men and women who would make their mark on the world. As we learn more and more about them, we continue to marvel at their accomplishments. We enjoy their works of art and literature. And we acknowledge that their beliefs, their actions, and their lives led to the world we know today. These men and women would make—and change—history.

Ramses II

Table of Contents

A GOLDEN JUBILEE 8

THE BIRTH OF AN EMPIRE 14

THE BOY WHO WOULD BE KING 28

NEW KING FOR A NEW KINGDOM 34

SOLE RULER OF EGYPT 46

WARRIOR KING 54

RAMSES THE BUILDER 66

RAMSES AND THE EXODUS 76

THE DEATH OF A PHARAOH 84

LIFE AND TIMES 96

LIFE AT A GLANCE 102

ADDITIONAL RESOURCES 103

GLOSSARY 105

SOURCE NOTES 107

SELECT BIBLIOGRAPHY 108

INDEX 109

IMAGE CREDITS 112

1 A GOLDEN JUBILEE

༄༅

The sun shone bright and hot in the clear blue sky as the crowd gathered. Streamers and pennants fluttered in the breeze. Men, women, and children chattered excitedly as they waited for the Heb-Sed festival to begin. For most Egyptians, witnessing a Heb-Sed Festival was a once-in-a-lifetime event.

A hush fell over the crowd as a procession entered the courtyard, built especially for the occasion. First came the priests, led by the high priest of Ptah, the king's son Khaemwaset. Then came the pharaoh himself, Ramses II, whom the people considered a living god. As their king passed, his subjects threw themselves face down and touched their heads to the ground.

Ramses approached a special platform across

Historians consider Ramses II to be one of the greatest pharaohs to have ruled ancient Egypt.

The hieroglyphic language of the ancient Egyptians does not include vowel sounds. Therefore, modern translators have to supply the vowels and can only guess at the proper spelling and pronunciations of names and other words. For this reason, every ancient Egyptian name can be found with multiple spellings, depending on the vowels each translator supplies. This adds to the confusion that already exists in the records. For example, the most powerful god in Egypt can be spelled Amen-Re, Amun-Re, or Amon-Ra.

from the audience. On it were two thrones representing Upper and Lower Egypt. To either side were shrines to various important gods. Ramses made offerings at the shrines before being led to a pavilion where the priests presented him with the crowns of Upper and Lower Egypt.

Ramses returned from the pavilion and faced his people. Dressed only in a short kilt and cloak, he was a sight to behold. Not yet 50 years old, the pharaoh was a great warrior who had led Egypt for 30 years. The crowd cheered as Ramses shot four arrows into the bright blue sky. The arrows soared off to the north, south, east, and west, frightening off evil spirits and reinforcing Egypt's right to rule the rest of the world.

As the priests began to chant, offering their praise to the pharaoh and thanks to the gods, Ramses removed his cloak. In his hand, he held his crook and flail and the *imyt per*—the written legacy that gave him the right to rule. The most important part of the festival was about to begin.

*Wennefer, a
high priest
under Ramses II,
is depicted
wearing a lion
skin and an
insignia that
symbolized
his position.*

Ramses made his way to a special track called "the
field." He ran around the boundary of the field four
times as the ruler of Upper Egypt and four times as the
ruler of Lower Egypt. This ritual was meant to renew
the king's powers and to prove that he was physically

Some animals in ancient Egypt were considered gods. The powerful bull was especially important because it symbolized the pharaoh's physical strength, fighting spirit, and brave heart. The Apis bull was the best known of the bull gods and could be identified at birth by very distinct markings. This black calf was said to have the image of an eagle on its back, a white diamond on its forehead, and the mark of a scarab (a dung beetle— a symbol of rebirth) under its tongue. It also had twice the normal amount of hairs on its tail. Egyptians celebrated the birth of an Apis calf because it signified that a living god had been born among them.

able to continue to rule the land. In many depictions of this run, the pharaoh is shown alongside the Apis bull, which further illustrates the king's might.

The Heb-Sed Festival, also known as the royal jubilee or simply the Sed festival, was very important in ancient Egypt. Traditionally, a pharaoh's first jubilee was to be held in the 30th year of his reign and then every two or three years thereafter. Not many pharaohs ruled long enough to celebrate a Sed festival—unless they bent the rules by holding the jubilee before reaching the 30-year mark.

Ramses II celebrated his first Sed in the 30th year of his reign and went on to celebrate 13 more over the course of his 67-year rule. But this is not the only area in which Ramses outshone Egypt's other pharaohs, truly earning his title "Ramses the Great." According to Rita Freed, the curator of the department of ancient Egyptian, Nubian, and Near Eastern Art at the Museum of Fine Arts in Boston:

So numerous and impressive are the contemporary records ... of [Ramses'] long reign and his many accomplishments, that history has recognized him as Ramesses the Great, the king whose name, in the thirteenth century B.C., inspired fear and awe throughout most of the known world.

As a pharaoh, Ramses' name appeared in a cartouche—an oval that surrounds the hieroglyphs of a king's or queen's name.

In the years after his death, many pharaohs would take the name of Ramses, perhaps hoping to recapture a little of the ancient king's legendary spirit. But as history has proved, there was only one Ramses the Great. ॐ

2 THE BIRTH OF AN EMPIRE

Egypt was not always ruled by a pharaoh such as Ramses. During the time before pharaohs, which is called the predynastic period, most Egyptians belonged to tribes and lived in villages. The villages belonged to independent districts or territories, which were ruled by chiefs.

In addition to tribal districts, there were also city-states in predynastic Egypt. Each city-state was made up of a town and the surrounding countryside. It was ruled by a king who had about the same amount of authority as a tribal chief.

City-states were formed when one village became more powerful than others in the area. After the village chief extended his influence over the neighboring villages, a city-state was born. This process

As an Egyptian king, Seti I—Ramses' father—had several names, including Meryenptah, Menmaatre, and Sethos.

continued until Egypt was made up of just two king-doms: Lower Egypt and Upper Egypt.

In about 3100 B.C., Menes—the king of Upper Egypt—conquered Lower Egypt and united the country. Egypt had become a nation, and Menes—also known as Narmer—was its first king. This is

King Narmer founded the first Egyptian dynasty by uniting Upper and Lower Egypt.

why Ramses ran around the field four times for Upper Egypt and four times for Lower Egypt during the Heb-Sed Festival. He was celebrating the unification of Egypt and asserting his right to rule the entire land.

For 3,000 years after Lower and Upper Egypt became united, the country would be ruled by kings, who were later called pharaohs. The pharaoh was considered a living god by his subjects and therefore had absolute power over every aspect of Egyptian life—from politics to religion.

Religion was very important to the ancient Egyptians, who worshipped many gods and goddesses. Some gods took a human form, others were animals, and still others were a combination of the two. The Egyptians believed that each of their gods had control over some aspect of everyday life.

The word pharaoh *did not originally apply to the king. The king's royal palace was known as the* per aa, *or "great house." Because he was thought of as a living god, ancient Egyptians considered it rude to refer to the king by name. Instead of talking about "the king," the people talked about the "great house." Per aa was later adapted by ancient writers as* pharaoh, *a name for the king.*

In about 2655 B.C., an era known as the Old Kingdom began. The pharaohs of this period created a system of government that would stay in place for the entire history of ancient Egypt.

The pharaoh was the head of state, and below

him was the vizier. The vizier oversaw Egypt's agriculture and irrigation systems, police and justice systems, and construction projects. The vizier was also in charge of the government treasury. He collected taxes and distributed the funds to pay for state projects, such as pyramid building.

Traditionally, the position of pharaoh was passed down from the reigning king to his oldest son. Many early rulers traced their ancestry to pharaohs who traced their roots to a god. This changed with the start of the 19th dynasty.

Ramses I, who was Ramses II's grandfather, did not have royal blood. He was the son of a soldier. Ramses I followed in his father's footsteps by starting his career as a soldier. He quickly became a favorite of Horemheb, the last king of the 18th dynasty. In fact, Horemheb appointed Ramses I vizier and named him co-regent (co-ruler).

Horemheb ruled for about 20 years at the end of the 18th dynasty.

Historians believe that Horemheb died without any sons. Since he had no sons to take his place as

A pharaoh was often depicted in the company of gods or goddesses. This emphasized his status as a descendant of the gods.

pharaoh, he named Ramses I as his heir and successor. Because Ramses I was not related to any kings of the 18th dynasty—nor had he married into a king's family—his reign marked the beginning of a new dynasty.

Ramses I came to the throne relatively late in

Ramses I's reign was so brief that his tomb was only partially constructed at the time of his death. It is unclear where the pharaoh's mummy rested because his tomb had been robbed before its discovery in 1817. Most of the contents—including his mummy—were most likely stolen by tomb robbers. What is thought to be Ramses I's mummy resurfaced in 1881 in America, where it was placed on display in the Niagara Museum and Daredevil Hall of Fame in Canada. The mummy found a new home at the Michael C. Carlos Museum in Atlanta, Georgia, in 1999 before being returned to Egypt in 2003.

life. He was probably in his 50s, which was old by ancient Egyptian standards. Though he reigned for less than two years (1292–1290 B.C.), Ramses I left behind a great legacy. His son Seti I and grandson Ramses II would go on to make the 19th dynasty (also known as the Ramesside period) one of the greatest in Egyptian history.

Ramses II's father, Seti I, became pharaoh in about 1290 B.C. During Seti's reign, ancient Egyptian arts and culture reached an all-time peak. The building projects that Seti oversaw included the great Hypostyle Hall in the Temple of Amen at Karnak, the temple at Abydos, and his tomb, which is considered one of the finest in the Valley of the Kings.

The Valley of the Kings is an area on the west bank of the Nile River across from Luxor, which in ancient times was called Waset. The tombs found here are all located underground instead of in pyramids. This is where most of the rulers of Egypt's New Kingdom were buried, including Ramses II.

From the time of the 3rd dynasty, pharaohs had built pyramids to house their tombs. But it is believed that the last pharaoh to do this was Ahmose, the first king of the 18th dynasty. By the time of Ramses' reign, the building of pyramids had been abandoned. Instead, pharaohs had their tombs built underground in a place known as the Valley of the Kings.

Seti followed in his father's military footsteps and greatly increased Egypt's might and influence

A limestone relief near Karnak shows Seti I defeating his enemies.

Everything scholars know about the Hittite Empire comes from ancient writings and excavations. It seems that the civilization first developed around 1900 B.C. in Anatolia, an area that covers modern-day Turkey and northern Syria. The Hittites' influence grew over 300 years until they became a true empire in about 1680 B.C. Hittite civilization is divided into three kingdoms—Old, Middle, and New. During the New Kingdom (c. 1400–1193 B.C.), the Hittites were the most powerful empire in the world. The Hittite civilization is also famous for its advanced system of government and military.

in the area. In his first year as pharaoh, Seti led an expedition into Syria, where he secured the main trade route along the coast of Gaza for Egypt. Later he led his troops against the Hittites in Syria and Lebanon. (The Hittite Empire was centered in Anatolia, which is in present-day Turkey.) A scene on the temple at Karnak shows Seti's army capturing the town of Kadesh. Years later, Ramses II would fight his most famous battle there.

Seti married Tuya, a woman who also came from a military family. The couple's first-born son died young. Their second son, Ramses II—the boy who would be king—was born in 1304 B.C.

Because Ramses II lived and ruled more than 3,000 years ago, it is hard to know exactly what his day-to-day life was like. It is even hard to know the exact dates of when historic events took place. However, thanks to the work of archaeologists—along with the written artifacts that ancient Egyptians left behind—there is a lot we do know about this civili-

In falcon form, the god Horus watches over Ramses II as a child.

zation. The three most important sources for information about ancient Egypt are written accounts, monuments (such as temples, tombs, and statues), and works of art.

The written language of ancient Egypt is one of

The word hieroglyphs comes from the Greek words meaning "sacred carvings."

the oldest in the world. Called hieroglyphs, the writing system was established as early as 3400 B.C. and continued in use until the fourth century A.D. The last dated hieroglyphs were written in 394 A.D. In hieroglyphic writing, pictures are used to represent letters, sounds, or whole words.

Many written accounts are found on papyrus—an early form of paper—or on ostraca, which are pieces of broken pottery or fragments of limestone. These accounts detail important events such as religious ceremonies and funeral practices, but they also include everyday documents, such as letters, school lessons, and lists.

Much of what we know about ancient Egypt also comes from tombs—structures that were built to contain a person's mummy and any possessions he or she might need in the afterlife. Some famous tombs are in the pyramids found at Giza in Egypt. Other famous tombs have been found in the Valley of the Kings.

Osiris was a powerful god of ancient Egypt and the first pharaoh of the land. After Osiris was killed by his brother Seth, Egyptians believed he was brought back to life by his wife Isis. Even though he was a god, Osiris could not return to the land of the living. He became the god of the underworld.

The story of Osiris gave ancient Egyptians a strong belief in life after death. That is why the Egyptians took great pains to make sure they would have everything they needed when they reached the afterlife. These preparations were very expensive, which is why peasants did not have such elaborate burial places.

For thousands of years, no one knew how to read hieroglyphs. Then, in 1799, the discovery of the Rosetta Stone finally unlocked the mystery of this ancient system of writing. The Rosetta Stone is a fragment of a second century B.C. basalt slab that contains engraved text in three scripts: hieroglyphs, the common Egyptian script (Demotic), and Greek. After comparing the hieroglyphs with the Greek translations, scholars were able to reconstruct the hieroglyphic alphabet and use it to read the texts decorating Egypt's monuments.

Tombs were decorated with murals and carved reliefs. Many of the tomb's decorations were religious in nature, but some murals showed scenes from a family's life. Items buried with a mummy also give clues to the type of life that person led. Household items, weapons, and tools have been found, as have

Reliefs, such as those on the columns of the Hypostyle Hall, provide insight into ancient Egyptian culture and history.

games and toys. These artifacts, which are thousands of years old, have survived because of Egypt's hot, dry climate.

Although artifacts found in the Egyptian sand can tell archaeologists a lot about ancient times, they cannot come close to presenting a complete picture. For example, statues found in tombs can give us an idea of what style of dress or hair was worn by ancient Egyptians, but they do not really tell us what the people looked like. These sculptures and murals often present "idealized" versions of real life, rather than an actual portrait. In other words, statues of Ramses do not depict what he really looked like. They are meant to show what the perfect ruler would look like. It is only by examining Ramses' mummy that archaeologists are able to get a glimpse of the real man who ruled Egypt. ல

A relief is a type of sculpture where the forms and figures exist on a different plane from the background. The forms can either be raised from the background (bas-relief) or carved into the background (sunken relief). A bas-relief is more time-consuming than a sunken relief. For a bas-relief, the artisan sketches out the figures and then carves away at the background until it is lower than the figures. For a sunken relief, the artisan carves the figures directly into the surface of the stone (or other material, such as wood).

3 THE BOY WHO WOULD BE KING

When he was 10 years old, Ramses received the title of "King's Eldest Son." He was also appointed commander in chief of the army.

Because the oldest son of the pharaoh was destined for the throne, Ramses' training began early. He would have learned archery, how to ride a horse, and how to drive a chariot. There was a lot of emphasis placed on physical fitness. In those days, the king did not give orders from a safe distance—he rode at the front of his army. It was crucial that the pharaoh be able to fight well. Military matters were of great concern to the pharaohs of the 19th dynasty.

For many years, Egypt's geographic location kept the country safe from attack. Deserts surrounded the Nile Valley to the east and west, and the

Mediterranean Sea formed the country's northern border. The tribes that lived to the south of Egypt were easily defended against.

During this time, Egyptian culture was able to flourish. The country's written language was expanded, and funds from taxation were funneled into projects such as the building of pyramids and monuments. The country did not have a full-time standing army until the start of the New Kingdom in 1550 B.C.

Even though the threat of a foreign invasion was

Despite their names, Lower Egypt was located north of Upper Egypt.

Mediterranean Sea

Tyre

Jerusalem

Tanis (Djanet)

Lower Egypt

Memphis

ASIA

Upper Egypt

Thebes (Luxor)

Syene (Aswan)

Nile River

Red Sea

AFRICA

Kush

Napata

Meroë

Tigris River

Euphrates River

N
W — E
S

0   300 miles

0   300 kilometers

Egypt, 1300 B.C.

small, Egypt did have an up-and-down history because of civil problems. The country was too large to govern easily, and on several occasions, Egypt's central government fell apart. During these times—known as "Intermediate Periods" (or the times between dynasties)—Egypt broke into smaller independent regions or kingdoms.

It is hard to determine exactly when these periods occurred. The calendar as we know it was not invented yet. The reign of a new king started a new year, and that "calendar" ended with his death. However, historians have divided ancient Egyptian history into three kingdoms: the Old Kingdom (2655–2176 B.C.), the Middle Kingdom (2130–1624 B.C.), and the New Kingdom (1550–1070 B.C.). Each kingdom is separated by an Intermediate Period.

It was not until the 18th century B.C. that the people of Egypt were forced to fight outside threats. This was during the Second Intermediate Period, between the end of the Middle Kingdom and the beginning of the New Kingdom.

At this time, the country was invaded by a people known as the Hyksos. Historians are not absolutely sure who the Hyksos were—the name can be translated from the Egyptian *hekau khasut*, which means "princes of foreign countries." However, we do know that these invading princes came from present-day Syria and Palestine, an area known to the ancient Egyptians as Retenu.

Perhaps the Hyksos merely came looking for grazing land or to trade with the Egyptians. Regardless of what their initial motives were, though, the invaders ultimately waged war on the Egyptians.

The Egyptians were outmatched in their fight against the Hyksos. The Hyksos were skilled fighters, and the Egyptians were not. While their enemies wore body armor, used advanced bows, and fought from chariots, the Egyptians went into battle without helmets and fought with inferior weapons, such as spears and axes.

From the late 1700s B.C., the Hyksos had political control of Egypt. The 15th and 16th dynasties belonged to the Hyksos, but the Egyptians benefited from their rule. Through their exposure to the Hyksos and their ways of fighting, the Egyptians were able to adopt the Hyksos' military technology. They, too, began using horse-drawn chariots and advanced bows.

By the end of the 17th dynasty, the Egyptians were able to defeat the Hyksos. Ahmose, an Egyptian, made himself ruler of Upper and Lower Egypt. The country was once again united under an Egyptian pharaoh.

However, there was a big difference between this pharaoh and those who had come before. Ahmose created a military state. A new age of imperialism was about to begin in Egypt. It was the start of the New Kingdom. For the first time, Egypt would have a professional army. And for the first time, starting under

the reign of Seti and reaching a peak under Ramses II, the country would become an international power.

From the time he was a young boy, Ramses II spent almost all of his time with his father, preparing for the day he would be named pharaoh. Reliefs from Karnak show Seti's military campaigns and the teenage Ramses alongside his father. By the time he was 22 years old, Ramses would lead his father's army south to put down a rebellion in Nubia. Like his grandfather and father before him, Ramses would be a great warrior. In fact, he would become famous as one of Egypt's greatest warrior kings. ✺

Seti I is shown making offerings to the gods. Some Egyptologists believe the person behind him is Ramses II, which would indicate that Ramses was next in line for the throne.

4 NEW KING FOR A NEW KINGDOM

Chapter

❧

In the seventh year of his reign, Seti named Ramses co-regent. Although Ramses' family probably took great pride in their military achievements, it was still important that the pharaoh distance himself from his "common" roots. Perhaps because his family lacked a royal bloodline, Seti was worried that someone might question Ramses' right to the throne.

Ramses' name now became Usermaatre Setepenre Ramses, which means "the justice of Re is powerful, born of Re." Re, the sun god, was one of the Egyptians' most important gods. The people believed that their king was one of Re's descendants. This new name, which emphasized Ramses' connection to Re, was one way to show that Ramses was the true pharaoh. To further emphasize the point, Ramses

A colossal monument of Ramses II at the temple at Karnak includes a smaller figure of his wife, Nefertari.

commissioned a stele at Abydos, which illustrated his divine birthright. A stele is a stone or wooden slab that is used as a memorial, to mark boundaries, or record historical events. The inscription reads:

> *It was Menmaatre (Seti) who nurtured me, and the All-Lord himself advanced me when I was a child until I could start to rule. Already when I was in the egg he had given the land to me. The officials kissed the ground before me when I was installed as the Eldest Son ... and when I reported concerning the affairs of the Two Lands [Upper and Lower Egypt] as a commander of the infantry and of the chariotry. When my father rose up before the people (when I was still a child in his arms) he said of me: "raise him as a king so that I may see his beauty while I still live."*

Even though he was the grandson of a common soldier, Ramses was proclaiming to the world that he had been born of a god as befitted the pharaoh.

In addition to being commander in chief of the army, Ramses was also given the title of Supervisor of All Constructions. It was clear from early on that he shared his father's interest in building projects.

The young man is mentioned in inscriptions that describe him overseeing the quarrying of stones for monuments and starting his own building projects. A stele at Quban describes Ramses' responsibilities: "No monument was raised that was not under your authority, no mission took place without your approval."

Ramses had another reason for building many temples. The pharaoh was the country's chief priest and was responsible for caring for the images of Egypt's gods, which were kept inside the temples. The Egyptians believed that when the images were well cared for, the gods themselves would inhabit them. Therefore statues of the gods were treated with great care

Ramses II offers incense to a shrine containing a statue of the god Amen.

and reverence. They were regularly washed, anointed with oils and perfumes, and presented with offerings.

In reality, it would be impossible for the pharaoh to care for the many holy images throughout the country. That job fell to individual priests who acted as representatives of the pharaoh. One way the pharaoh serviced the gods was by building magnificent temples throughout Egypt. The more temples and statues that existed of a god, the more that god was honored.

The ancient Egyptians believed that if they took good care of their gods, the gods would return the favor by making sure the people had enough food to eat, among other things. In fact, every ancient Egyptian could see proof that the gods were happy any time they looked at the Nile River.

For thousands of years before Ramses' birth, ancient Egyptians considered the Nile River and the sun to be the sources of all life. The Nile enabled the Egyptians to build a thriving country in the middle of the desert. Most of the estimated 1 million people who lived in ancient Egypt lived in a region of about 12,500 square miles (32,500 square kilometers). This was the land along the narrow floodplain on either side of the Nile River. It included parts of the Nile Delta, which they were able to farm. This region accounted for only about 3 percent of the country's total area. The rest of the area was desert.

An ancient Egyptian hymn shows the importance of the Nile:

Running for 4,160 miles (6,656 km), the Nile River is the longest river in the world.

> *Hail to thee, O Nile! Who manifests thyself over this land, and comes to give life to Egypt! Mysterious is thy issuing forth from the darkness, on this day whereon it is celebrated! Watering the orchards created by Re, to cause all the cattle to live, you give the earth to drink, inexhaustible one!*

Ancient Egyptians planned their lives around the Nile—it was the source that enabled them to grow crops in the desert. Every year, from June to September, the river would flood. When the flood-waters receded, farmers would scatter their seeds into the mud that was left behind. Ancient Egyptian farmers planted barley, wheat, and various fruits and vegetables.

Although the flooding of the Nile was fairly predictable, it was still a cause for great anxiety. If the waters rose too high, a farmer's land could be destroyed. If the waters did not rise high enough, there would not be enough water to sustain the farmer's crops.

To ensure the success of their crops, ancient Egyptian farmers built a sophisticated irrigation system. Reservoirs were dug into the ground to catch floodwaters. Canals were then dug to carry the water from the reservoirs to the fields. Farmers built dikes to reinforce the reservoir walls. The water in the reservoirs could continually provide water for the farmers' crops—even in those fields that were far from the banks of the river.

Most of the people in ancient Egypt were farmers. They did not own the land, however. Farmers worked the fields for a landlord—usually the pharaoh.

A farmer's life was not easy. Building and repairing dikes, digging canals, plowing the land, planting

A painting from the 19th dynasty depicts Egyptian agricultural methods.

seeds, and harvesting crops were hard work. All of this strenuous labor did not yield much income for the farmer and his family.

During late summer, when the land was flooded, farmers often turned to other work, such as building projects and handicrafts. However, farmers could be called from their land at any time to join the army or work on state projects, such as constructing royal tombs or temples. When this happened, the pharaoh provided food for the farmer and his family.

Farmers were not the only Egyptian citizens to work part time for the pharaoh. Contrary to popular belief, there were very few slaves in Egypt. Regular Egyptians did most of the hard work of digging ditches and hauling stones for building projects on their duty days.

When Ramses became co-regent, he moved into his own palace. In addition to the part-time laborers who worked on the palace, Ramses employed a large staff to take care of his growing family. At the same time Ramses moved into his palace, he received his first two wives.

Ramses' wives Nefertari and Istnofret were both beautiful and intelligent. Ramses would go on to have eight wives in total, as well as a large harem, but Nefertari was his chief wife and constant companion until she died in year 24 of his reign. Scholars also believe that she was the love of his life.

As principal wife, Nefertari held a high status during Ramses' reign. Experts believe she was also revered for her beauty and charm. As with her husband, ancient Egyptians considered Nefertari a living god. A description of the queen, found in text carved on a wall in Luxor Temple, read:

Greatly favoured, possessing charm, sweet of love ... rich in love ... singer fair of face, beautiful with the tall twin plumes, Chief of the Harim of Horus, Lord of the Palace; one is pleased with what comes forth concerning her; who has [only to] say anything, and it is done for her—every good thing, at her wish; her every word, how pleasing on the ear—one lives at just hearing her voice.

Nefertari wore the elaborate vulture crown of an Egyptian queen.

Nefertari was the mother of Ramses' first-born son, Amenhirkhopshef, and at least three other sons and two daughters. Istnofret gave birth to three sons: Ramses, Khaemwaset, and Merenptah. Istnofret's Ramses was not the one who would one day rule Egypt as Ramses III; he died before his father—Ramses II—and therefore never took the throne.

Ramses' son Khaemwaset has been called the first "Egyptologist" because he identified and restored many historic buildings and artifacts.

Ramses' other wives included Henutmire, who was his younger sister, as well as three of his daughters: Bint-Anath, Nebettawy, and Meryetamen. Ancient Egyptians saw no problem with royal relatives marrying each other. They believed that intermarriage helped keep the divine bloodline pure. Ancient Egyptians were also imitating the god Osiris, who married his sister Isis. Their son Horus was the protector of Egypt's pharaoh. In fact, all of Egypt's rulers were given the title Living Horus as one of their names.

Nefertari, the Great Royal Wife, was the most powerful woman in the land. Ordinarily, it was her son who would become pharaoh. However, Nefertari's sons all died before their father. If a pharaoh's principal wife did not have any sons, her daughter could be married to the son of one of the pharaoh's secondary wives. It was Merenptah, son of Istnofret, who would succeed Ramses II as pharaoh.

Ramses also added two Hittite princesses as wives later in his reign. The first was named Maathorneferure, but the name of the second is unknown. It has been estimated that Ramses fathered more than 100 sons and daughters.

5 SOLE RULER OF EGYPT

᎒᙮᙮᙮᎒

When Seti died around 1279 B.C., Ramses II became the sole ruler of Egypt at age 25. Ramses had learned at Seti's feet, and his father had selected his best advisers to help groom and serve Ramses as pharaoh. Ramses' mother, Tuya, was still alive, and she also probably served as an adviser to the pharaoh.

As soon as Ramses took the throne, he announced that he was moving the capital of Egypt from Memphis. He was building a new city near Avaris to be called Pi-Ramesse Aa-nakhtu, which means "house of Ramses—great of victories."

This move fed Ramses' appetite for building, but it also served a military purpose. In addition to the palaces and temples that filled the city, Pi-Ramesse also served as a garrison. The many troops stationed there were on constant alert to stop any threats from crossing Egypt's eastern borders.

It is hard to know exactly what the royal family's life was like in the capital city of Pi-Ramesse. Unlike temples and other monuments, which were made of stone, homes were made of wood and mud bricks. Therefore, the materials did not last through the centuries, and little remains to study. However, some scholars have been able to reconstruct what Ramses' life was probably like.

The royal family lived in a great palace in the middle of the city. The rooms of the palace did not contain a lot of furniture, but they were beautifully decorated. The walls, ceilings, and floors would have been painted with scenes from daily life. There might have been scenes of Ramses hunting with his sons or leading his troops into battle painted on the walls. Paintings on the ceilings might have shown the night sky over Egypt.

Each member of the family had his or her own suite of rooms, which was furnished with elaborately carved and decorated furniture. There were chairs with feet in the shape of lions' paws and chests for clothes that were made of ebony and inlaid with gold and ivory.

Every morning Ramses started his day by bathing in an alabaster tub, a morning ritual that was watched by several important guests, as well as the

Nefertari is depicted playing senet, an Egyptian game similar to backgammon.

pharaoh's servants. For invited guests, taking part in the pharaoh's morning routine was considered a great honor.

After his bath, Ramses would have been visited by his barber. Ancient Egyptians strongly believed in neatness and good hygiene. The men, therefore, were almost always clean-shaven. The only times Egyptian men went without shaving were when they were in mourning or traveling abroad. This is at odds with the ancient Egyptian belief that the gods had beards. So although Ramses was clean-shaven, on special occasions, he would have worn a fake beard attached by a cord to show his status as a living god.

Although they did not like body hair and did everything they could to eliminate it, the Egyptians took great pride in the hair on their heads. Ramses' servants would have spent hours braiding the family's hair, possibly weaving gold charms and jewels into their locks. Perhaps, like many Egyptians, Ramses shaved his head in favor of elaborate wigs. Nefertari might have had extensions woven into her hair as well.

The queens and princesses wore long, form-fitting gowns, while Ramses and his sons wore pleated kilts. Both the gowns and kilts were made of fine linen and decorated with gold thread. The men and women all wore heavy eye makeup and exquisite jewelry, including necklaces, bracelets, rings, and anklets made of precious metals and stones. Ancient Egyptians believed that these pieces of jewelry provided spiritual protection to the wearer.

When he finished dressing, Ramses would have put on his crown or other headgear and gathered his flail and crook. The flail and crook were types of scepters, or symbols of authority, and were carried mainly during ceremonial occasions.

The flail was a rod that had three beaded strands

attached. It is hard to know for sure, but it was probably modeled on a shepherd's whip or fly whisk. Such a scepter would have symbolized the pharaoh's role as guardian, or shepherd, of his people.

The crook was a cane that had a hooked handle. This scepter was probably modeled after a shepherd's staff. The crook was often gold plated and decorated with blue bands. The meaning of the hieroglyphic crook sign was "ruler" or "to rule."

Ramses' name appears in the cartouche found on an elaborate pendant decorated with images of the vulture and cobra goddesses.

Prior to 3000 B.C., there were two crowns for Egyptian kings. The king of Upper Egypt wore a white crown, and the king of Lower Egypt wore a red crown. After Egypt's unification, the king wore the double crown, which was known as the "Two Mighty Ones."

By the time of Ramses' rule, the pharaoh is often depicted wearing a blue crown, which is also known as the war crown. This tall helmet is decorated with golden disks and has a Uraeus and vulture on the brow. The Uraeus, a symbol of kingship, is a serpent emblem, usually considered a cobra. According to legend, the god Geb gave the cobra to the pharaohs as a sign of kingship. The Uraeus is intended to protect the pharaoh by spitting fire at his enemies. Another royal symbol is the vulture, a symbol of the goddess Nekhbet, protector of the pharaoh.

Ramses might also have worn the Nemes Crown, which is really more of a headdress. The headdress was made from a piece of striped cloth that was pulled tightly across the head and tied in back. Two pieces of the cloth hung down on the sides of the pharaoh's head, and the brow was decorated with the Uraeus.

When Ramses was fully dressed, he went to the throne room to conduct business. Here he conferred with his advisers and met with people who came to petition him for help. Later, he and Nefertari would

Some statues of Ramses show him wearing the double crown of Upper and Lower Egypt, as well as a pharaoh's false beard.

sail up and down the Nile visiting other parts of the kingdom. Little by little, the great warrior was increasing the size of Egypt's empire. ✍

WARRIOR KING

Chapter
6

Ramses II is a name that has echoed through the ages for many reasons. He was one of the longest-reigning pharaohs. In fact, his reign lasted longer than many ancient Egyptians lived. In a time when large harems and numerous children were common for rulers, Ramses had more wives and children than anyone before or after him. He also built more temples and monuments than any other Egyptian pharaoh.

However, it is probably Ramses' incredible military might that earned him the name "Ramses the Great." Over the course of his long reign, Ramses fought many battles to regain territory that previous pharaohs had lost. His most famous battle was the battle of Kadesh, which was fought in the fifth year of his reign.

In the battle of Kadesh, Ramses II's army consisted of chariots, archers, and possibly lions.

From the time of Seti I's reign, a truce had existed between the Egyptian pharaoh and the Hittite king Mursilis II. For several years, there was peace in the region. After the two kings died, though, the truce was broken. It was only a matter of time before violence broke out in the region once again.

The Battle of Kadesh was sparked by the desire of both the Egyptians and the Hittites to expand their empires.

In year five of his reign (1274 B.C.), Ramses faced the new Hittite king, Muwatallis, in a battle for the city of Kadesh. Details of the battle were recorded on temples and monuments throughout Egypt and

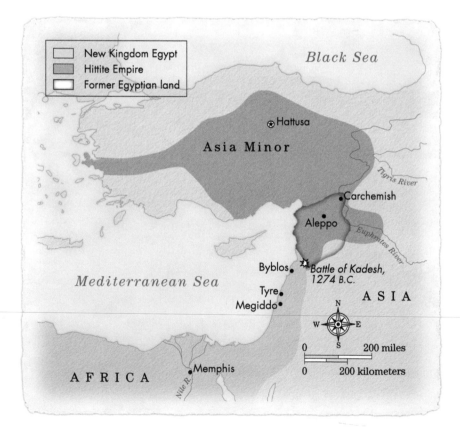

New Kingdom Egypt
Hittite Empire
Former Egyptian land

Black Sea

⊗ Hattusa

Asia Minor

Tigris River

●Carchemish

Aleppo
●

Euphrates River

Byblos●
☆ Battle of Kadesh,
1274 B.C.

Mediterranean Sea

Tyre●
Megiddo●

ASIA

N
W ⊕ E
S

0   200 miles
0   200 kilometers

●Memphis

AFRICA

Nile R.

Syria. Each side tells a slightly different version, but one thing is certain: Though Ramses was a good strategist and an excellent warrior, the battle of Kadesh nearly ended in disaster for the young pharaoh.

Ramses commanded a force of 20,000 men broken into four divisions of 5,000 each. The divisions were named after the gods Amen, Re, Ptah, and Seth. Each division contained chariots, archers, and infantry. Ramses himself rode at the head of the Amen division.

The majority of Ramses' troops were Egyptian. But there were also foreign soldiers in the army. They were mainly Libyan and Sherden prisoners who had been forced into military service. Muwatallis led an even greater force: two sections of about 19,000 men each plus 2,500 chariots.

In the spring of 1274 B.C., Ramses and his army marched east toward Kadesh through Gaza, Canaan, and Syria. When he got to Lebanon, Ramses sent a task force to move up the coast and secure a port. Upon reaching the outskirts of Kadesh, the pharaoh and the rest of his troops stopped to make camp in the woods.

Amen and Re were both sun gods and creator gods. Re was closely linked to the king and Egyptian kingship. Ptah was another of the creator gods. He was the patron of craftsmen and the most important deity of the city of Memphis. Seth was responsible for the death of Osiris—his brother. After killing Osiris, Seth tried to take his brother's position as the king of the gods. Ultimately, though, Seth—who was also the god of chaos—was defeated.

A fierce warrior, Ramses rode at the front of his troops when he led his army into battle.

While they were patrolling the woods, Egyptian guards found two men who claimed to be Hittite soldiers. They said they had deserted the Hittite army and wanted to serve the pharaoh. The men said that the Hittite army was camped about 20 miles (32 km) north of Kadesh. However, these men were not deserters at all. They were spies who had come to give the Egyptians false information and lead them into a trap.

Ramses, wanting to seize the element of surprise, led his Amen division across the Orontes

River, where they set up camp far from the rest of his army. As his soldiers prepared Ramses' traveling throne so he could scout the city, the pharaoh's guards captured two more men. They were obviously Hittite spies and were reluctant to give the Egyptians any information. After a brutal interrogation, they confessed that "Lo! The king of Hatti has already arrived ... they stand armed and ready for battle behind the old city of Kadesh."

Ramses quickly sent a runner to alert his other three divisions. But just as the Re division was emerging from the woods—still about 5 miles (8 km) south of the Amen camp—the Hittite chariots tore through their ranks. Before the Egyptian soldiers could even draw their bows, they were cut down by the enemy's spears. Those that survived scattered, mostly toward the Amen camp, and the Hittite soldiers followed.

It is believed that Ramses' army contained hired soldiers who were probably paid based on how many of the enemy they killed. Archaeological records show the grotesque accounting method used to count the soldiers' accomplishments: They would cut the right hand from their fallen enemy to present to Ramses as proof of each kill.

The pharaoh and his soldiers were taken by surprise. Several Egyptian reliefs that depict the battle show the Egyptians watering their horses and repairing their equipment at one end of the camp while the

Hittite chariots are breaking through the fence at the other end. No sooner did the Hittites arrive, though, than most of the Amen division ran away. Only Ramses and his personal guards were left behind.

Temple inscriptions record Ramses' reaction as his troops scattered in fear. The great warrior appealed to Amen:

> *I call to you, my father Amun,*
> *I am among a host of strangers;*
> *All countries are arrayed against me,*
> *I am alone, there's none with me.*
> *My numerous troops have deserted me,*
> *Not one of my chariotry looks for me;*
> *I keep on shouting for them,*
> *But none of them heeds my call.*
> *I know Amun helps me more than*
>   *a million troops,*
> *More than a hundred thousand charioteers,*
> *More than ten thousand brothers and sons*
> *Who are united as one heart ...*
> *I found Amun came [w]hen I called to him,*
> *He gave me his hand and I rejoiced.*

Then Ramses quickly put on his armor, mounted his chariot, and charged directly into the midst of the enemy. In an attempt to rally his remaining men, the king cried out, "Stand firm, steady your hearts my army. That you may behold my victory, I am alone, but Amun will be my protector, his hand is with me."

Rather than crushing the Egyptians, the Hittite

troops paused in the attack to ransack the camp. At the same time, the task force that had separated from Ramses' troops in Lebanon rejoined the army. They turned the tables, joining Ramses in his attack on the

Many experts consider the battle of Kadesh to be the high-light of Ramses' military campaigns.

Several reliefs recorded the details of Ramses' courage during the battle of Kadesh.

Hittites. A bloody hand-to-hand battle was in full force when the Ptah division made it to the camp and joined the rest of the troops. Before nightfall, the Egyptians pushed the Hittites back to the Orontes River.

The next morning, neither king was eager to resume the fighting. Muwatallis sent a letter to

Ramses that read, in part: "Do not be hard in your actions, victorious king, peace is better than fighting, give us time to breathe." Though no peace treaty was signed that day, there was no more fighting. Both armies returned home, each claiming victory.

For his part, Ramses had accounts of the battle inscribed on temples and monuments across Egypt. All of them claimed absolute victory for Egypt—brought about almost single-handedly by Ramses.

A Hittite version of the battle also exists. This version claims that Ramses was defeated and forced to retreat, giving up territories in northern Syria that Seti I had claimed. Neither account is completely true, but for several years the cease-fire remained in effect.

Relations between the two kingdoms began to break down in about year eight of Ramses' reign. King Muwatallis died, and in the struggle for power that followed, Muwatallis' brother Hattusilis took

The Hittite capital of Hatti was located in Hattusa. When King Muwatallis II took the throne in 1295 B.C., he moved the capital to Tarhuntassa and appointed his brother Hattusilis governor of Hattusa. During this time, Hattusilis conquered Nerik, a city north of the Hittite capital, and made himself one of the city's high priests. When Muwatallis died in 1272 B.C., his son Muwatallis III became king. Muwatallis III moved the capital back to Hattusa, which left Hattusilis no city to govern. He also removed his uncle from his position as a high priest of Nerik. These events triggered a civil war, which Hattusilis won. After seizing the crown from his nephew, Hattusilis sent him into exile.

Ramses' sons accompanied their father on the battlefield at a young age.

the throne. Hattusilis, a warrior, would have loved the opportunity to invade Egypt.

The Egyptians and Hittites continued to fight over the years, constantly battling for control of northern Syria. But hostilities never escalated to the level of the battle of Kadesh. Then, in about year 20, a new threat brought these old enemies together.

The Assyrians were gaining power in the area, overthrowing established empires and getting ready to invade Hatti. Hattusilis knew it would be in his country's best interest to form an alliance with Egypt.

In year 21, the two kingdoms signed a peace treaty, which was inscribed on two matching silver tablets and copied onto the walls of the temple at Karnak and the Ramesseum (Ramses' funerary temple). The treaty represented a promise that the two nations would never go to war again. It also stated that they would come to the other's aid as necessary.

The former enemies were now allies. Twelve years after signing the treaty, Hattusilis deepened the relationship between the two nations by sending his daughter to Egypt as a bride for Ramses. Several years later, in 1239 B.C., a second Hittite princess joined the harem.

As peace settled once again over Egypt, Ramses was free to pursue his other passion: building. With fewer men needed to fight in far-off lands, Egyptian citizens could dedicate themselves to the pharaoh's many construction projects.

The Egyptian-Hittite peace treaty was not the first in history. However, it is the oldest surviving treaty for which a full record exists. Amazingly, both the Egyptian and Hittite copies have been found. The Hittite version was recorded on clay tablets that were later found in the capital city of Hattusas. Not surprisingly, the Hittite version of the treaty does not match the Egyptian version. The Egyptians claim that the Hittites asked for peace. The Hittites claim it was the other way around.

7 RAMSES THE BUILDER

❧⨯❧

Commissioning building projects was an important part of a pharaoh's duties, especially when his subjects and state funds were not tied up in warfare. Ramses began construction projects from the start of his reign—most notably the city of Pi-Ramesse and his funerary temple. But Egypt's new period of peace led to a boom in construction.

From the time he was a young boy, Ramses took a great interest in building. He watched his father commission monuments throughout his kingdom, and he even oversaw construction on some of Seti's temples himself. Ramses knew that pharaohs were judged by the number of monuments that bore their names, as well as how elaborate their funerary temples were. Historians can tell which pharaoh built certain

Some of Ramses' most impressive monuments were obelisks— towering, four-sided structures covered with hieroglyphs.

Every monument a pharaoh had built showed honor to the gods. It also increased the status of the king. Every monument was a display of the pharaoh's wealth and power—as well as his religious devotion. In fact, many monuments featured statues of the pharaoh and his family along with representations of the gods. At the very least, the monument contained the name of the pharaoh who had commissioned it. Building temples was time-consuming work, though. Often, in addition to building new monuments, a pharaoh would claim the monuments of earlier kings for themselves. The pharaoh would simply have the previous ruler's cartouche chiseled out and replaced with his own.

monuments by the cartouche that is found there.

An even more important reason for building temples and monuments was to keep Egypt's many gods satisfied. Egyptians believed that the gods controlled every aspect of their lives. If the gods were happy, Egypt would prosper. On the other hand, if the gods were unhappy, Egypt would erupt into chaos. The pharaoh was the link between the gods and his people, which is why the commissioning of temples was one of his more important responsibilities.

Although Ramses' vizier, Paser, oversaw the day-to-day progress at the construction sites, the pharaoh clearly took an interest in the process. A stele found in the Red Mountain quarries records how he identified a block of stone to use for a statue of himself. It also details how he looked after his workers by giving them food, drink, and clothing.

Over the course of his 67-year reign, Ramses ordered the construction of more temples and monuments than any pharaoh before or after him. He had no way of knowing that he would live and reign for such a long time. To complete as many monuments as he could, the pharaoh had his artisans create a new style of relief. Up until this time, sculptors created bas-reliefs for the temples and monuments. In an effort to save time, Ramses had his sculptors use sunken relief.

Ancient Egyptians had a strong belief in the afterlife, so the construction of a pharaoh's tomb was very important. Sculptors carved protective prayers into the walls of the tombs to ensure a safe journey to the

Although bas-reliefs allowed for more detail than sunken reliefs, they were also more time consuming.

underworld for their pharaoh. Anything the pharaoh might need in the afterlife—including furniture, jewelry, weapons, and games—was buried with him for use after death.

Workers began constructing Ramses' tomb in the Valley of the Kings in year two of the pharaoh's reign. For 20 years, more than 100 laborers and their families lived in a village known as the Place of Truth while they worked on the project. The village was located in the desert outside of Waset—close to the Valley of the Kings.

At the time, the location of the Valley of the Kings was kept secret to protect the tombs from grave

The Valley of the Kings is the location of more than 60 tombs.

robbers. The people who lived in the Place of Truth were the only commoners who knew of its existence. Though they were isolated, the workers and their families were well taken care of. Paser made sure that their shipments of food and beer were always on time. They had good houses to live in.

Archaeologists found an inscription in the workmen's village. It was written by a scribe called Ramose and recorded his instructions from Paser:

> Now the city prefect and vizier Paser has written me saying, "Please have the wages delivered to the necropolis crew comprising vegetables, fish, firewood, pottery, small cattle, and milk. Don't let anything thereof remain outstanding. [Don't] make me treat any part of their wages as balance due. Be to it and pay heed!"

At the start of the week, the craftsmen and laborers would march to the worksite with their tools and equipment. They would stay in huts at the site and work for eight days, then return to their families in the village and get two days off.

Constructing a tomb was hard work. First, stonecutters had to make a tunnel in the side of a cliff. Then they smoothed out the rock walls so that they could be decorated. Sculptors carved reliefs into the walls, which were then brightly painted. Every bit of the wall was covered with scenes. Some scenes

The entrance to many Egyptian temples and palaces of the New Kingdom featured pylons—huge stone towers—that were covered in hieroglyphs. Directly behind the pylon entrance was an open court that led to the temple. The hall was the outermost and most elaborate part of the temple.

depicted the pharaoh's life and achievements, while others were taken from important religious texts and stories. The reliefs contained pictures as well as hieroglyphic writings. This process was repeated on the many rooms inside the tomb.

Not surprisingly, Ramses' tomb is one of the largest in the Valley of the Kings. It covers more than 8,800 square feet (792 square meters). Unfortunately, Ramses' tomb has not survived well. Its location has been flooded many times, so most of the paintings that covered the walls have been destroyed. Since the tomb has been open since ancient times, most of the treasures that were buried with the pharaoh have long since disappeared.

Before the New Kingdom, pharaohs had their mortuary temples built close to their royal tombs. A mortuary temple was a place where priests could perform rites for the benefit of the dead ruler. By the time of Ramses' rule, pharaohs had their mortuary complexes built farther from their tombs, so Ramses' survived.

Called the Ramesseum, Ramses' complex was gigantic, measuring about 984 feet (300 m) long and 640 feet (195 m) wide. It included a tremendous pylon entrance, a palace, a great Hypostyle Hall, a sanctuary, and even a small town that housed the priests, scribes, and others needed in service of the site.

All around the complex were reliefs depicting Ramses' achievements. One whole wall was dedicated to his victory at the battle of Kadesh, while others showed his devotion to the gods and to his family.

Just inside the first court stood a colossal statue of the king, which stood 55 feet (16.8 m) tall and weighed 1,000 tons (900 metric tons). Penra, Ramses' architect, designed the complex facing east so that the sun's first rays would light up the statue of the king.

A giant statue of Ramses II is displayed in its own building in an Egyptian museum in Memphis, Egypt.

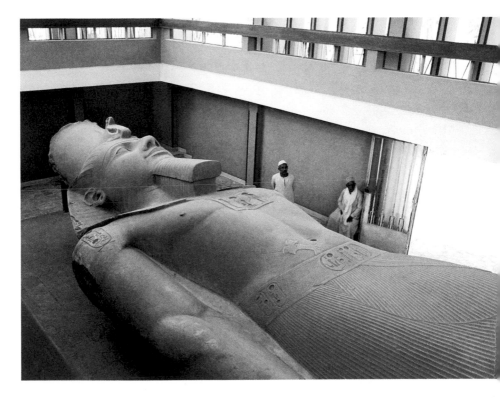

Even more amazing than the Ramesseum are the temples that Ramses built at Abu Simbel in Nubia. The outside of the Great Temple features two pairs of statues of Ramses seated on either side of the entrance that are 65 feet (19.8 m) high. At his feet are smaller statues of his family.

The main temple was cut into the side of a cliff to a depth of 200 feet (61 m). The temple was constructed so that on February 20 and October 20, the rising sun would reach the sanctuary 200 feet inside the mountain and shine on three of the four gods seated there. Only the statues of Amen-Re, Re-Harakhte, and Ramses felt the rays of the sun. The statue of Ptah, who was a god of the underworld, fittingly remained in darkness.

In addition to the Great Temple, Abu Simbel also included a smaller temple that Ramses built to honor Nefertari. Though he constructed many monuments to his beloved wife, this temple is probably the greatest. Outside the temple are two statues of Nefertari, with statues of Ramses on either side.

In 1952, Egypt's president announced plans to build the Aswan High Dam across the Nile in order to control the river's floodwaters. The dam would create a lake (Lake Nasser) that would cover the temples at Abu Simbel. The United Nations Educational, Scientific, and Cultural Organization (UNESCO) stepped in to save the site. Between 1964 and 1968, the entire site was cut into blocks, moved to a spot 213 feet (65 m) higher and 656 feet (200 m) back from the river, and reassembled.

Several statues of Ramses, Nefertari, and some of their children adorn the entrance of the magnificent Hathor Temple in Abu Simbel.

Smaller statues of their children are located near Nefertari's and Ramses' feet. An inscription there reads: "He had this temple cut into the mountain, an eternal work, for his principle wife, Nefertari, beloved of Mut [queen of the gods], for all eternity, Nefertari, for whom the sun doth shine."

The dedication of both temples took place in year 24 of Ramses' reign (1256 B.C.). Nefertari died soon after. The tomb that Ramses commissioned for her is the finest in the Valley of the Queens, an area like the Valley of the Kings but reserved for the wives of the pharaohs. 🙰

8 RAMSES AND THE EXODUS

❧⟨✕⟩❧

With all of the construction going on during Ramses' reign, the pharaoh would have required a huge work-force. Although the work was difficult, Egyptians felt it an honor to work on projects such as their pharaoh's tomb or his great new city of Pi-Ramesse. Likewise, letters from the time tell us that many peasants sought to leave farming for a better life as a shopkeeper or servant in the city.

Still, it was difficult to find enough construction workers for all the projects. It is likely that tribes-men from Sinai who wandered into the area would have been enslaved and forced to work for the pha-raoh. Some scholars suggest this is what happened to the Hebrews.

The presence of the Hebrews in Egypt, particularly

According to the Bible, Moses parted the Red Sea and led the Israelites through the wilderness to escape from bondage in Egypt.

77 ↘

as slave laborers in Pi-Ramesse, is the basis for the story of the Exodus in the Bible. This, and other archaeological evidence, leads some scholars to believe that Ramses was the pharaoh from that story. They think that the Exodus occurred sometime during the years 20 to 30 of Ramses' reign.

According to the Bible, Moses—as a representative of the Hebrews' God—went to the pharaoh and ordered him to release his people from bondage.

Moses pleaded his case before the pharaoh.

When the pharaoh refused, God punished him and his people with 10 plagues. The final plague, according to tradition, resulted in the death of the pharaoh's firstborn son.

The Bible relates that it was the death of his son that finally convinced pharaoh to set the Hebrews free. However, after the king's huge workforce left the city, the pharaoh regretted his decision and led his army to recapture the fleeing slaves. The Hebrews made their final escape—as recorded in the Bible—when Moses parted the Red Sea. After the Hebrews walked across the dry seabed, the waters crashed down upon the trailing Egyptian chariots.

Today, some scholars believe they have the facts to explain this miraculous escape. *Yam Suf*, which has traditionally been translated as "Red Sea," means "sea of reeds." It is likely that this refers to the marshlands found in eastern Egypt. These marshlands lie along the route that, according to the biblical account, was taken by

According to the Bible, the plagues visited upon Egypt were:

1. *All the waters of Egypt turning to blood*
2. *The country being overrun by frogs*
3. *Gnats covering the land*
4. *Swarms of flies invading Egypt*
5. *Livestock becoming diseased*
6. *Boils appearing on all of the Egyptians and their livestock*
7. *Giant thunder and hailstorms*
8. *A swarm of locusts covering the earth*
9. *Three days of darkness*
10. *The death of all firstborn Egyptian children*

the fleeing Hebrews. Though people on foot could have made it safely across such marshlands, chariots would have gotten mired in the soft ground.

Archaeological records confirm that Ramses and Nefertari's firstborn son Amenhirkhopshef died before inheriting the throne. Until recently, though, it was not known how or when he died.

For 3,000 years, the location of the prince's final resting place was a mystery. Then, in 1994, Egyptologist Kent Weeks made a startling discovery— what he believed to be the tomb of Amenhirkhopshef.

The tomb, which has been labeled KV5, is thought to be the biggest and most complex ever found in Egypt. It is believed to house 50 of Ramses' sons, including Amenhirkhopshef. Paintings found in the tomb show Ramses presenting several of his newly deceased sons to various gods. Hieroglyphs above the paintings indicate that Amenhirkhopshef is one of the sons being presented.

The skull that Weeks believes belongs to

Kent Weeks is the director of the Theban Mapping Project, an organization dedicated to preserving the ancient Egyptian tombs in Thebes.

*Tomb KV5
in Thebes*

Amenhirkhopshef is that of a mature young man, not a child. It seems to indicate that a blow to the head—not a plague or curse—caused the prince's death. Nevertheless, Amenhirkhopshef's death might still be tied to the Exodus.

It is likely that between the years 20 and 30 of his reign, Ramses no longer rode at the head of his army. He had accomplished great things and, by the

Kent Weeks had been studying the area near Tomb KV5 in the Valley of the Kings since 1978, when he started what is now called the Theban Mapping Project. The project, which was only supposed to last a few seasons, was heading into its second decade when Weeks discovered KV5. By that time, Egyptian officials believed there was nothing left to discover on the site and were getting ready to build a parking lot there. Weeks wanted to make sure the parking lot would not destroy any important artifacts, so he decided to explore the area one last time. It was then that he found the tomb—one of the largest in the world.

age of 50, had settled into his role as a living god. Scholars believe that Amenhirkhopshef became commander in chief of the army. Therefore, it is possible that Amenhirkhopshef pursued the Hebrews to the sea, not Ramses.

The Bible states that Moses was in "mixed company," meaning that some of the Hebrews were armed. It is possible that the Hebrews ambushed the Egyptian soldiers, whose chariots were stuck in the mud, killing Amenhirkhopshef. The idea that Ramses' firstborn was struck down by God could refer not to a plague, but rather to the Hebrews acting as agents of God.

It is hard to know what happened for sure, since the Egyptians left no record of this event. This is not surprising, though. Pharaohs chose only to leave behind stories of their achievements.

No matter how Amenhirkhopshef died, it was sure to have devastated Ramses, who built his son's tomb just 100 feet (30.5 m) from his own. Ramses would bury

many of his wives and children during his long life. But it would be more than 30 years before Ramses the Great would join his loved ones in the afterworld. ☙

Amenhirkhopshef and Ramses II are featured together in several reliefs, showing the importance of the pharaoh's firstborn son.

RAMÉSSE II
DN. XIX. 1351-1823. a.C.

9 THE DEATH OF A PHARAOH

❧

In year 67 of his reign (1212 B.C.), when he was about 92 years old, Ramses II died. He was ready to make his journey to the afterlife. The pharaoh had lived an incredibly long life—the average ancient Egyptian only lived to about 35 or 40 years old. Still, the loss of such a great ruler must have been met with incredible despair and mourning. For many of his subjects, Ramses was the only ruler they had ever known.

Ramses' tomb had been ready for years, and now it was up to the priests to see Ramses safely to the next world. Ancient Egyptians believed that a pharaoh's soul would need its body in order to complete its journey to the afterlife. If the body were allowed to decay, the pharaoh's spirit (called *ka*) would be forced to wander alone for eternity. In order to

Ramses' military campaigns, building projects, and long reign made him one of the most successful pharaohs of ancient Egypt.

85 ◈

Ramses, who ruled until his death at age 92, was the oldest pharaoh in history.

preserve the pharaoh's dead body, they developed the process of mummification.

After Ramses died, servants carried his body to a tent known as the *ibu*, or place of purification. The priest embalmers laid him on a table, washed his body with palm oil, and rinsed it with water from the Nile. Then they made a cut in Ramses' left side and removed his internal organs. His liver, lungs, stomach, and intestines were washed and packed in natron, a type of salt used to dry out the organs. Then the organs were usually placed in containers called canopic jars.

By the time of Ramses' death, canopic jars were closed with stoppers shaped like the heads of a baboon, a human, a jackal, and a falcon. These represented the four children of Horus. The deceased's lungs were placed in the baboon-headed jar. The liver was placed in the jar with the human-head stopper. The stomach and upper intestines were stored in the jackal-headed jar, and the lower intestines were placed in the jar with the falcon-head stopper.

The four gods represented as stoppers on canopic jars were Duametef (jackal), Hapy (baboon), Imsety (human), and Qebehsenuef (falcon).

Archaeologists found a set of blue glazed canopic jars that they believed belonged to Ramses II. Later scientific studies, however, showed that these jars did not contain Ramses' remains. The pharaoh's true canopic jars have never been found.

Ordinarily, the pharaoh's heart would not have been removed along with the other organs. Egyptians believed that the heart was the center of the soul. The

87

Egyptians believed that after Osiris was killed, Anubis embalmed the god and wrapped his body, creating the first mummy. Anubis, a jackal-headed god, was one of Osiris' sons and lived with his father in the underworld. Anubis was the god who determined which souls he would lead to the court of Osiris for their final judgment.

heart would also be required to testify on pharaoh's behalf during the weighing of the heart ceremony in Osiris' court. This ceremony was presided over by Anubis, the god of embalming. During the ceremony, Ramses' heart would be weighed to determine whether he had led a good life. Only those who passed the test would be taken to Osiris, the god of the underworld, to be judged.

Ramses' embalmers accidentally removed his heart during the embalming process. They corrected their mistake by sewing the organ back inside the pharaoh's body.

Next, the embalmers took a long hook and inserted it into Ramses' nose to remove his brain. Then they filled his nasal cavity with peppercorns. This was not a usual practice and explains why Ramses' mummy is one of the few with such a distinctive profile. The noses on most mummies are flattened by the wrappings.

Once his organs were removed, the embalmers again washed Ramses' body and filled it with incense and perfumes before stitching it closed. Then they covered his body with natron so that every last bit of moisture would be removed and his body would not decay.

After 70 days, the priests rubbed Ramses' dried-up body with perfumed oils and wrapped it in strips of fine linen. The priests started with Ramses' head

Mummification was a practice reserved for pharaohs and the wealthy.

The Book of the Dead, which was known to ancient Egyptians as peret em herew (coming forth by day), is a funerary text. It contains spells and instructions to help the deceased pass through the underworld and reach a happy afterlife in the Field of Reeds. The Book of the Dead contains almost 200 texts, which are divided into individual spells. Spells were often written on sheets of papyrus and placed with the dead to help them on their journey. The spells could also be written on tomb walls, pieces of linen, or on the coffin of the deceased. During the Ramesside Period, most of the magical texts were accompanied by illustrations. The opposite had been true in earlier periods, when the texts contained few illustrations.

and neck, and then they individually wrapped his fingers and toes. His arms and legs were wrapped separately and then tied together. A papyrus scroll inscribed with spells from the *Book of the Dead* was placed between Ramses' hands, and more linen strips were wrapped around his body.

The second layer of wrappings was soaked in resin and sweet-smelling oils so that the strips would stick together. Embalmers placed amulets (charms) between the layers of wrappings to protect Ramses' body on its journey to the underworld. Finally, a cloth was wrapped around the pharaoh's body and painted with a picture of Osiris. During the wrapping process, a priest read spells out loud to protect Ramses from evil spirits and help him on his journey.

In preparation for Ramses' funeral, his mummy was laid in a coffin, which was then laid inside two progressively larger coffins. Finally, all three were enclosed

Writings in the Book of the Dead *were often used in funeral rituals.*

in a larger coffin called a sarcophagus. After being transferred to the royal barge, Ramses' body traveled down the Nile. During the three-week journey from Pi-Ramesse to Waset and the Valley of the Kings, people crowded the banks of the Nile to pay their respects to the pharaoh. The air was filled with the sounds of crying and wailing, as women threw sand over their heads and tore at their clothes.

After arriving in Waset, Ramses' sarcophagus was pulled on a wooden sledge to his tomb. Priests led the way, while Ramses' family and other mourners followed behind. Servants brought up the rear,

> The Egyptians wanted to honor their pharaoh as befitted a living god. However, they had other motives for ensuring his successful journey to the afterlife. They believed that once the pharaoh arrived in the next world, he would ensure the safety of his people.

carrying the furniture, food, weapons, and other items Ramses would need in the next life.

At the entrance to the tomb, Ramses' son and successor Merenptah performed the opening of the mouth ceremony. This ceremony was intended to restore Ramses' senses and give him the ability to eat and drink.

Then the priests laid Ramses inside a stone sarcophagus deep in his tomb. No one was allowed to enter the pharaoh's tomb, so the doors were sealed shut. The priest ended the ceremony by reciting a prayer that ensured the pharaoh would find new life in the afterworld. He stated that Ramses would be young again and would remain so throughout eternity. Then, as the last mourners left the tomb, they swept away their footprints behind them.

Ramses' mummy did not spend eternity in his tomb as intended. It was discovered along with other royal mummies in Deir el Bahri in 1881. According to records found with the body, Ramses' tomb had been robbed in ancient times. After that, his mummy had been moved twice for protection. In about 1054 B.C., it was moved to his father's tomb. It is not known at what point it was taken to its final resting place in Deir el Bahri.

A wooden coffin case of Ramses II depicts him holding the crook and the flail—symbols of kingship.

In 1976, Ramses' mummy took another trip—this time to Paris, France, where it was examined and placed on exhibit. Despite the fact that the pharaoh had been dead for more than 3,000 years, he received a king's welcome at the Paris airport, where his mummy was greeted by a full presidential honor guard.

X-rays of Ramses' mummy showed that he had a long, narrow, oval-shaped face and a rather large nose. He was 5 feet 8 inches (173 centimeters) tall—which was quite large for a time when the average height was 5 feet 3 inches (160 cm). His hair was red.

Ramses' mummy is on display at the Egyptian Museum in Cairo.

The examination also showed that Ramses suffered from many ailments that can be associated with advanced age. He had severe tooth and gum decay

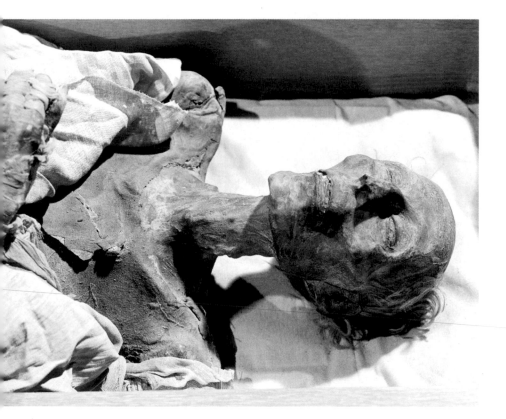

and several large cavities. He also suffered from circulatory problems and arthritis of the hip. These health problems, along with the fact that Ramses out-lived Nefertari and most of his children, must have made the last years of the pharaoh's life quite diffi-cult and sad. Nevertheless, what the world remem-bers of Ramses the Great is just what the pharaoh would have wanted. According to Rita Freed:

> *In our own century, more than 3,000 years after his death, Ramesses the Great still earns universal respect. His monu-ments still evoke a sense of awe, and the world still pays him homage. ... Today looking down from his large temple [at Abu Simbel], four 65-foot-high, seated statues of Ramesses II, with wives and children at his feet, dominate the Nile. Ramesses the Great has gained immortal-ity. His greatness lives on.* 𝕾

RAMSES II'S LIFE

1304 B.C.
Ramses II is born

1300 B.C.

1300 B.C.
Aryans migrate into
the Indus Valley

1400 B.C.
Iron Age begins in
Asia Minor

WORLD EVENTS

1279 B.C.

Seti I dies; Ramses becomes sole ruler of Egypt

1283 B.C.

Ramses II is named co-regent to his father, Seti I

1280 B.C.

1280 B.C.

The Torah is believed to have been fully composed

RAMSES II'S LIFE

1274 B.C.

Ramses fights in
the battle of Kadesh

1270 B.C.

1274 B.C.

Shalmaneser
becomes king of the
Assyrian Empire

1270 B.C.

Syrian scholar
compiles an
encyclopedia

WORLD EVENTS

1259 B.C.

Ramses signs historic
peace treaty with the
Hittites

1258 B.C.

Ramses' mother,
Tuya, dies

1260 B.C.

1257 B.C.

Slánoll rules as
high king of Ireland
until 1241

RAMSES II'S LIFE

1256 B.C.

The Temples at Abu Simbel are dedicated

1250 B.C.

Ramses celebrates his first Sed festival

1255 B.C.

Queen Nefertari dies; Istnofret becomes Ramses' principal wife

1250 B.C.

1250 B.C.

The Greeks and Trojans fight the Trojan War, as described in Homer's *Iliad*

1254 B.C.

Kudur-Enlil rules Babylon until 1245

WORLD EVENTS

1212 B.C.

Ramses dies; his
son Merenptah
succeeds him
as pharaoh

1230 B.C.

Myceneans
conquer Troy

1220 B.C.

Assyrians capture
Babylon

1226 B.C.

First recorded
eruption of
Mount Etna

DATE OF BIRTH:	1304 B.C.
BIRTHPLACE:	Probably Memphis
FATHER:	Seti I
MOTHER:	Tuya
SPOUSES:	Nefertari
	Istnofret
	Bint-Anath
	Meryetamen
	Nebettawy
	Henutmire
	Maathorneferure (1st Hittite princess)
	Name unknown (2nd Hittite princess)
CHILDREN:	Ramses is thought to have had more than 100 children
DATE OF DEATH:	1212 B.C.
PLACE OF DEATH:	Probably Pi-Ramesse

FURTHER READING

Cline, Eric H., and Jill Rubalcaba. *The Ancient Egyptian World*. New York: Oxford University Press, 2005.

Rees, Rosemary. *The Ancient Egyptians*. Chicago: Heinemann Library, 2006.

Tyldesley, Joyce. *Egypt*. New York: Simon & Schuster Books, 2007.

Whiting, Jim. *The Life & Times of Rameses the Great*. Hockessin, Del.: Mitchell Lane Publishers, 2005.

LOOK FOR MORE SIGNATURE LIVES BOOKS ABOUT THIS ERA:

Alexander the Great: *World Conqueror*

Aristotle: *Philosopher, Teacher, and Scientist*

Confucius: *Chinese Philosopher and Teacher*

Hatshepsut: *Egypt's First Female Pharaoh*

Hypatia: *Mathematician, Inventor, and Philosopher*

Julius Caesar: *Roman General and Statesman*

Socrates: *Ancient Greek in Search of Truth*

Thucydides: *Ancient Greek Historian*

On the Web

For more information on this topic, use FactHound.

1. Go to *www.facthound.com*
2. Type in this book ID: 075653836X
3. Click on the *Fetch It* button.

FactHound will find the best Web sites for you.

Historic Sites

Egyptian Museum
Midan El Tahrir
Cairo, Egypt
202/578-2448
Mummies, jewelry, ancient Egyptian papyrus, and other artifacts

The Metropolitan Museum of Art
1000 Fifth Ave.
New York, NY 10028
212/535-7710
Temples, sculptures, jewelry, and other artifacts

anointed
applied oil or a similar substance to something

artifacts
objects created or used by humans from a
particular time period

canopic jars
containers used to hold a mummy's internal organs

cartouche
oval that surrounds the hieroglyphs of a king's or
queen's name

crook
scepter shaped like a cane with a hooked handle

dikes
barriers built to control or hold water

flail
scepter shaped like a rod with three beaded
strands attached

garrison
military post

hieroglyphs
writing system in which pictures are used to
represent letters, sounds, or whole words; hiero-
glyphics is used to describe the type of writing

imperialism
one nation gaining power or control over
other nations

irrigation
using artificial means to water land

ka
person's soul or spirit

legacy
something passed on to a person from his or
her ancestor

papyrus
early form of paper

pharaoh
ruler of Egypt

Osiris
supreme deity of the ancient Egyptians and lord of
the underworld

ostraca
pieces of broken pottery or fragments of limestone
on which written accounts are often found

Ramesseum
Ramses' mortuary complex; place where priests
could perform rites for the dead pharaoh

Ramesside Period
another name for the 19th dynasty

reservoirs
artificial lakes where water is collected and stored

scepters
staffs carried by rulers as symbols of authority

stele
stone or wooden slab that is used as a memorial,
to mark boundaries, or record historical events

Uraeus
serpent emblem, usually considered a cobra, that
is a symbol of kingship

Valley of the Kings
location of many ancient Egyptian tombs near
modern-day Luxor

Chapter 1

Page 13, line 1: Rita Freed. *Ramesses the Great.* Boston: Boston Museum of Science, 1988, p. 24.

Chapter 4

Page 36, line 5: Tony High. "The Life of Ramesses the Great." *Egyptology Online.* 14 Oct. 2007. www.egyptologyonline.com/the_life_of_ramessess_the_great.htm, p. 2.

Page 36, line 29: Ibid.

Page 39, line 3: Oliver J. Thatcher, ed. *The Library of Original Sources.* Milwaukee: University Research Extension, 1907, pp. 79–83.

Page 43, line 1: Kent Weeks. *The Lost Tomb.* New York: William Morrow, 1998, p. 207.

Chapter 6

Page 59, line 8: "The Life of Ramesses the Great," p. 5.

Page 60, line 8: *The Lost Tomb*, pp. 273–274.

Page 60, line 26: "The Life of Ramesses the Great," p. 5.

Page 63, line 1: Ibid.

Chapter 7

Page 71, line 10: *The Lost Tomb*, p. 46.

Page 75, line 3: "The Life of Ramesses the Great," p. 3.

Chapter 9

Page 95, line 9: *Ramesses the Great,* p. 118.

Clayton, Peter A. *Chronicle of the Pharaohs: The Reign-by-Reign Record of the Rulers and Dynasties of Ancient Egypt.* London: Thames & Hudson, 1994.

Freed, Rita. *Ramesses the Great.* Boston: Boston Museum of Science, 1988.

High, Tony. "The Life of Ramesses the Great." *Egyptology Online.* 14 Oct. 2007. www.egyptologyonline.com/the_life_of_ramessess_the_great.htm

Hobson, Christine. *Exploring the World of the Pharaohs.* London: Paul Press, Ltd., 1987.

James, T.G.H. *Ramses II.* New York: Friedman/Fairfax, 2002.

The Mysteries of Egypt: Ramses II. Cromwell Productions/Kultur Films, 1996.

Newby, P.H. *Warrior Pharaohs: The Rise and Fall of the Egyptian Empire.* Boston: Faber and Faber, 1980.

Rameses: Wrath of God or Man? Dir. Tom Pollack. Sony Pictures, 2005.

Reeves, Nicholas, and Richard H. Wilkinson. *The Complete Valley of the Kings: Tombs and Treasures of Egypt's Greatest Pharaohs.* New York: Thames & Hudson, 1996.

Roberts, Paul William. *River in the Desert: Modern Travels in Ancient Egypt.* New York: Random House, 1993.

Silverman, David, ed. *Ancient Egypt.* New York: Oxford University Press, 2003.

Thatcher, Oliver J., ed. *The Library of Original Sources.* Milwaukee: University Research Extension, 1907.

Velikovsky, Immanuel. *Ramses II and His Time.* Cutchogue, N.Y.: Buccaneer Books, 1978.

Weeks, Kent. *The Lost Tomb.* New York: William Morrow, 1998.

Abu Simbel, 74, 95
Abydos, 20, 36
Ahmose (pharaoh), 21, 32
Amen (god), 10, 39, 57, 60, 74
Amen (military division), 57, 58–59, 60
Amenhirkhopshef (son), 44, 80–81, 82
amulets, 90
Anubis (god), 88
Apis bulls, 12
Assyrians, 64
Aswan High Dam, 74
Avaris, 47

bas-reliefs, 27, 69
Battle of Kadesh, 55, 56–63, 64, 73
Bible, 78–80, 82
Bint-Anath (daughter), 45
Book of the Dead, 90

canopic jars, 86–87
cartouches, 68
city-states, 15–16

Deir el Bahri, 92
double crowns, 52

Egypt
    average lifespan in, 85
    calendar, 31
    capital of, 47–48, 67, 77, 78, 91
    city-states, 15–16
    climate of, 27
    construction projects, 18, 36, 42, 65,
        67, 68–70, 71–72, 74–75, 77
    dynasties, 18, 19, 20, 21, 29, 32
    farming in, 40–42
    Hebrews in, 77–80, 82
    hieroglyphic language, 10, 23–25,
        30, 51, 72, 80
    Hittites and, 22, 56–63, 64–65
    hygiene in, 49–50
    Hyksos and, 32
    Intermediate Periods, 31
    location of, 29–30
    Lower Egypt, 10, 11, 16, 17, 32, 52

Middle Kingdom, 31
military of, 21–22, 29, 32, 42, 55,
    56–63, 81–82
New Kingdom, 20, 30, 31, 32, 72
Old Kingdom, 17, 31
peace treaties, 65
predynastic period, 15
Ramesside period, 20, 90
slavery in, 42, 77, 78, 79
tribal districts, 15, 30
unification of, 16–17, 52
Upper Egypt, 10, 11, 16, 17, 52
viziers, 18, 68, 71
Exodus, 78–79, 81

Field of Reeds, 90
Freed, Rita, 12–13, 95
funerary temples. *See* mortuary temples.

grave robbers. *See* tomb robbers.
Great Temple, 74

Hattusilis (Hittite king), 63–64, 64–65
Hebrews, 77–80, 82
Heb-Sed Festival, 9–12, 17
Henutmire (wife/sister), 45
hieroglyphic language, 10, 23–25, 30,
    51, 72, 80
Hittite Empire, 22, 45, 56–63, 63–65
Horemheb (king), 18–19
Horus (god), 32, 45, 86
Hyksos, 31–32
Hypostyle Hall, 20, 73

ibu (place of purification), 86
imyt per (written legacy), 10
Intermediate Periods, 31
Isis (goddess), 45
Istnofret (wife), 42, 44, 45

ka (spirit), 85–86
Kadesh, 22, 55, 56–63, 64, 73
Karnak, 20, 22, 33, 65
Khaemwaset (son), 9, 44

Lake Nasser, 74
Lower Egypt, 10, 11, 16, 17, 32, 36, 52
Luxor, 20, 42. *See also* Waset.

Maathorneferure (wife), 45
Menes (pharaoh), 16–17
Merenptah (son), 44, 45, 92
Meryetamen (daughter), 45
Michael C. Carlos Museum, 20
Middle Kingdom, 31
monuments, 23, 25, 30, 36–37, 48, 55,
    56–57, 63, 67, 68–69, 74, 95
mortuary temples, 65, 67, 72
Moses, 78–79, 82
mummification, 86–90
murals, 26, 27
Mursilis II (Hittite king), 56
Muwatallis (Hittite king), 56, 57, 62–63
Muwatallis II (Hittite king), 63
Muwatallis III (Hittite king), 63

Narmer. *See* Menes.
natron (salt), 86, 88
Nebettawy (daughter), 45
Nefertari (wife), 42–44, 45, 50, 52–53,
    74, 75, 80, 95
Nekhbet (goddess), 52
Nemes Crown, 52
New Kingdom, 20, 22, 30, 31, 32, 72
Niagara Museum and Daredevil Hall of
    Fame, 20
Nile River, 20, 29, 38–40, 53, 74, 86,
    91, 95

Old Kingdom, 17, 31
Osiris (god), 25, 45, 57, 88, 90
ostraca (limestone fragments), 24–25

papyrus, 24–25, 90
Paser (vizier), 68, 71
Penra (architect), 73
Pi-Ramesse, 47–48, 67, 77, 78, 91
The Place of Truth, 70, 71
plagues, 79, 81, 82
Ptah division, 57, 62

Ptah (god), 57, 74
pylons, 72
pyramids, 18, 20, 21, 25, 30

Quban, 36–37

Ramesseum, 65, 72–73, 74
Ramesside Period, 20, 90
Ramose (scribe), 71
Ramses I (pharaoh), 18–20
Ramses II
    architect of, 73
    at Battle of Kadesh, 55, 56–63
    birth of, 22
    birthright of, 35–36
    canopic jars of, 87
    childhood of, 29, 33
    children of, 44, 45, 55, 75, 79, 80,
        82–83, 92, 95
    construction projects of, 36–37, 65,
        67, 68–69, 74, 77
    as co-regent, 35, 42
    death of, 85
    double crown of, 52
    Exodus and, 78
    father of, 20, 21–22, 33, 35, 36, 47,
        56, 63, 67
    flail and crook of, 10, 50–51
    funeral procession of, 91–92
    health of, 94–95
    heart of, 87–88
    at Heb-Sed festival, 9–12, 17
    height of, 94
    hygiene of, 48–50
    imyt per of, 10
    as "King's Eldest Son," 29
    military and, 21–22, 55, 56–63,
        81–82
    mortuary temple of, 67, 72–73
    mother of, 47
    mummification of, 86–90
    mummy of, 27, 92–95
    name of, 35
    Nemes Crown of, 52
    at Pi-Ramesse, 48–49, 52–53

statues of, 27, 68, 73, 74–75, 95
as Supervisor of All Constructions,
    36–37
tomb of, 20, 70–72, 85, 91–92
vizier of, 68, 71
war crown of, 52
wigs of, 50
wives of, 42–44, 45, 50, 52–53, 65,
    74, 75, 80, 82–83, 95
X-rays of, 94–95
Ramses III (son), 44
Re (god), 35, 39, 57, 60, 74
Re (military division), 57, 59
Red Sea, 79–80
Re-Harakhte (god), 74
reliefs, 26, 27, 33, 56–57, 59, 69,
    71–72, 73
religion
    afterlife, 25–27, 69–70, 85–86, 90,
        91–92
    Amen (god), 10, 57, 60, 74
    amulets, 90
    animals and, 12, 17
    Anubis (god), 88
    Book of the Dead, 90
    chief priests, 37
    facial hair and, 50
    "god images," 37–38
    Heb-Sed Festival, 9–12
    Horus (god), 43, 45, 86
    ibu (place of purification), 86
    Isis (goddess), 45
    ka (spirit), 85–86
    mummification, 86–90
    Nekhbet (goddess), 52
    Nile River and, 38
    Osiris (god), 25, 45, 57, 88, 90
    pharaohs and, 37–38
    priests, 9, 10, 37, 38, 63, 72, 73, 85,
        86, 89–90, 91, 92
    Ptah (god), 57, 74
    Re (god), 35, 39, 57, 60, 74
    Re-Harakhte (god), 74
    Seth (god), 57
Rosetta Stone, 25

royal jubilee. See Heb-Sed Festival.

sarcophagi, 91, 92
scarabs, 12
sculpture, 27
Second Intermediate Period, 31
Sed festival. See Heb-Sed Festival.
Seth division, 57
Seth (god), 57
Seti I (pharaoh/father), 20, 21–22, 33,
    35, 36, 47, 56, 63, 67
statues, 23, 27, 68, 73, 74–75, 95
stele, 36–37, 68
sunken reliefs, 27, 69

Temple of Amen, 20, 22, 33, 65
temples, 20, 22, 23, 37, 38, 42–43, 47,
    55, 56–57, 60, 63, 65, 67, 68–69,
    72, 74–75, 95
Theban Mapping Project, 82
Tomb KV5, 80–81, 82
tomb robbers, 20, 70–71, 92
tombs, 20, 21, 23, 25, 26–27, 42,
    69–72, 75, 77, 80, 82, 85, 91–92
Tuya (mother), 42, 47

United Nations Educational, Scientific,
    and Cultural Organization
    (UNESCO), 74
Upper Egypt, 10, 11, 16, 17, 52
Uraeus (symbol of kingship), 52

Valley of the Kings, 20, 21, 25, 70–71,
    72, 75, 82, 91
Valley of the Queens, 75
viziers, 18, 68, 71

war crowns, 52
Waset, 20, 70, 91. See also Luxor.
Weeks, Kent, 80–81, 82

Stephanie Fitzgerald has been writing nonfiction for children for more than 10 years. Her specialties include history, wildlife, and popular culture. Stephanie is currently working on a picture book with the help of her daughter, Molly.

Image Credits

Deejpilot/iStockphoto, cover (top), 4–5, 100 (top); Gianni Dagli Orti/Corbis, cover (bottom), 2; Jason Walton/iStockphoto, 8, 97 (top right); Erich Lessing/Art Resource, N.Y., 11, 28, 51; CJPhoto/iStockphoto, 13; Mary Evans Picture Library, 14, 16, 19, 61, 86; The Granger Collection, New York, 18, 23, 96 (top); The Print Collector/Alamy, 21, 81, 91; Federico Arnao/iStockphoto, 24; Jan Rihak/iStockphoto, 26; Jim Henderson/Alamy, 33, 97 (top left); Serge Vero/iStockphoto, 34; National Geographic/Getty Images, 37, 64, 93; Jakub Niezabitowski/Shutterstock, 39, 62; Interfoto Pressebildagentur/Alamy, 41, 44; Barry Iverson/Time Life Pictures/Getty Images, 43; Sandro Vannini/Corbis, 46; Werner Forman/Art Resource, N.Y., 49; Vladimir Korostyshevskiy/iStockphoto, 53, 101 (top); akg-images, 54, 98 (top); Mansell/Time Life Pictures/Getty Images, 58; Worldwide Picture Library/Alamy, 66; Phooey/iStockphoto, 69; Vova Pomortzeff/iStockphoto, 70; bygonetimes/Alamy, 73; Pierrette Guertin/iStockphoto, 75; North Wind Picture Archives, 76; Mary Evans Picture Library/Douglas McCarthy, 78; Barry Iverson/Time Life Pictures/Getty Images, 80; Roger Wood/Corbis, 83; Egyptian Museum, Turin, Italy/BEBA/AISA/The Bridgeman Art Library, 84; akg-images/Electa, 87; Mary Evans/Mary Evans ILN Pictures, 89; The Bridgeman Art Library/Getty Images, 94; Mundoview/Shutterstock, 96 (bottom); Greg McCracken/iStockphoto, 97 (bottom); Wikimedia/public-domain image, 98 (bottom), 101 (bottom left); Kelvin Wakefield/iStockphoto, 99; Vladimir Korostyshevskiy/Shutterstock, 100 (bottom); Govert Nieuwland/iStockphoto, 101 (bottom middle); Dimitry Romanchuck/iStockphoto, 101 (bottom right).